JOBS

by Robin Nelson

first step nonfiction

↳ Lerner Publications Company · Minneapolis

People need jobs.

A job is work we do.

People have jobs at school.

People have jobs at home.

People have jobs inside.

People have jobs outside.

We all have jobs.